Introduction

"The Owl and the Pussy-Cat went to sea
In a beautiful pea-green boat . . ."

The Owl and the Pussy-Cat are just two of the well known characters chosen by Marjorie Rogers and illustrated by Eric Kincaid to guide young people on a voyage of poetic discovery in *A Children's Book of Verse.*

It's a journey to carry their imaginations deep into a myriad of enchanting worlds; some familiar, others excitingly fresh and unknown. With the turn of every page, a different view opens up, changing from the wilds of the Scottish Highlands to Wordsworth's daffodil-strewn English Lake District and from the cowboy plains of the American West to the lost lands of Eldorado.

Showing the way are poets from across the centuries and from many different parts of the world; they include Keats, Burns and Tennyson, as well as modern masters such as Ogden Nash, Roger McGough and Spike Milligan. Their verses roam down the evergreen lanes of romance, adventure, heroism, villainy, magic and rib-tickling laughter.

Travel to the end of the rainbow, soar with eagles, fly to the moon, shiver with old Jack Frost, delight in the animal kingdom, tremble in the underworld, dance with the fairies at the bottom of the garden or watch the seasons change . . . with poetry there are no bounds to how far the young eye can see and Eric Kincaid's marvellous illustrations ensure the view is both clear and pleasing.

So, where did the Owl and the Pussy-Cat go?

"They sailed away for a year and a day
To the land where the Bong-Tree grows . . ."

Join them, and hundreds of other bewitching characters, on a spellbinding journey into the magical world of poetry.

ISBN 0 86112 426 X
© Brimax Books Ltd 1987. All rights reserved.
Published by Brimax Books Ltd, Newmarket, England 1987
Fourth printing 1990
Produced by Mandarin Offset
Printed and bound in Hong Kong

A
CHILDREN'S
BOOK OF
VERSE

Illustrated by ERIC KINCAID

Poems selected by MARJORIE ROGERS

BRIMAX BOOKS·NEWMARKET·ENGLAND

Contents

The Lonely Scarecrow

My poor old bones—I've only two—
A broomshank and a broken stave,
My ragged gloves are a disgrace,
My one peg-foot is in the grave.

I wear the labourer's old clothes;
Coat, shirt and trousers all undone.
I bear my cross upon a hill
In rain and shine, in snow and sun.

I cannot help the way I look.
My funny hat is full of hay.
—O, wild birds, come and nest in me!
Why do you always fly away?

James Kirkup

The Eagle

He clasps the crag with crooked hands;
Close to the sun in lonely lands,
Ring'd with the azure world, he stands.

The wrinkled sea beneath him crawls;
He watches from his mountain walls,
And like a thunderbolt he falls.

Alfred, Lord Tennyson

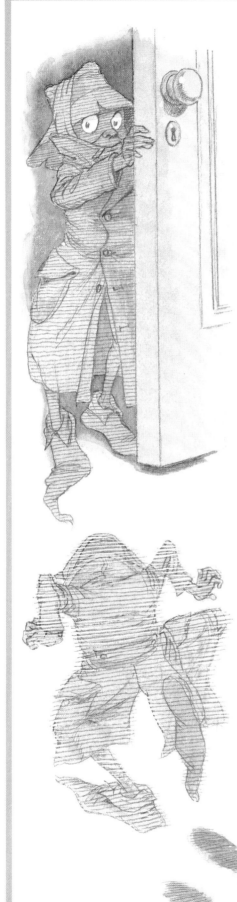

Mr Nobody

I know a funny little man,
    As quiet as a mouse,
Who does the mischief that is done
    In everybody's house!
There's no one ever sees his face,
    And yet we all agree
That every plate we break was cracked
    By Mr Nobody.

'Tis he who always tears our books,
    Who leaves the door ajar,
He pulls the buttons from our shirts,
    And scatters pins afar;
That squeaking door will always squeak
    For, prithee, don't you see,
We leave the oiling to be done
    By Mr Nobody.

He puts damp wood upon the fire,
    That kettles cannot boil;
His are the feet that bring in mud,
    And all the carpets soil.
The papers always are mislaid,
    Who had them last but he?
There's not one tosses them about
    But Mr Nobody.

The finger-marks upon the door
    By none of us are made;
We never leave the blinds unclosed,
    To let the curtains fade;
The ink we never spill; the boots
    That lying round you see
Are not our boots; they all belong
    To Mr Nobody.

Anonymous

The Highwayman

Part One

The wind was a torrent of darkness among the gusty trees,
The moon was a ghostly galleon tossed upon cloudy seas,
The road was a ribbon of moonlight over the purple moor,
And the highwayman came riding—
        Riding—riding—
The highwayman came riding, up to the old inn-door.

He'd a French cocked-hat on his forehead, a bunch
    of lace at his chin,
A coat of the claret velvet, and breeches of brown
    doeskin:
They fitted with never a wrinkle; his boots were
    up to the thigh!
And he rode with a jewelled twinkle,
        His pistol butts a-twinkle,
His rapier hilt a-twinkle, under the jewelled sky.

Over the cobbles he clattered and clashed in the
    dark inn-yard,
And he tapped with his whip on the shutters, but all
    was locked and barred:
He whistled a tune to the window, and who should
    be waiting there
But the landlord's black-eyed daughter,
        Bess, the landlord's daughter,
Plaiting a dark red love-knot into her long black hair.

And dark in the dark old inn-yard a stable-wicket creaked
Where Tim, the ostler, listened; his face was white
    and peaked,
His eyes were hollows of madness, his hair like
    mouldy hay;
But he loved the landlord's daughter,
        The landlord's red-lipped daughter:
Dumb as a dog he listened, and he heard the
    robber say—

'One kiss, my bonny sweetheart, I'm after a prize
    tonight,
But I shall be back with the yellow gold before the
    morning light.
Yet if they press me sharply, and harry me through
    the day,
Then look for me by moonlight:
        Watch for me by moonlight:
I'll come to thee by moonlight, though Hell should
    bar the way.'

He rose upright in the stirrups, he scarce could
    reach her hand;
But she loosened her hair i' the casement! His face
    burnt like a brand
As the black cascade of perfume came tumbling
    over his breast;
And he kissed its waves in the moonlight,
        (Oh, sweet black waves in the moonlight)
Then he tugged at his reins in the moonlight, and
    galloped away to the West.

Part Two

He did not come in the dawning; he did not come
   at noon;
And out of the tawny sunset, before the rise
   o' the moon,
When the road was a gypsy's ribbon, looping
   the purple moor,
A red-coat troop came marching—
      Marching—marching—
King George's men came marching, up to the
   old inn-door.

They said no word to the landlord, they drank
   his ale instead;
But they gagged his daughter and bound her to
   the foot of her narrow bed.
Two of them knelt at her casement, with muskets
   at the side!
There was death at every window;
      And Hell at one dark window;
For Bess could see, through her casement, the road that
   he would ride.

They had tied her up to attention, with many a
   sniggering jest:
They had bound a musket beside her, with the barrel
   beneath her breast!
'Now keep good watch!' and they kissed her.
      She heard the dead man say—
Look for me by moonlight;
   Watch for me by moonlight;
I'll come to thee by moonlight, though Hell should
   bar the way!

She twisted her hands behind her; but all the knots
    held good!
She writhed her hands till her fingers were wet with
    sweat or blood!
They stretched and strained in the darkness, and the
    hours crawled by like years;
Till, now, on the stroke of midnight,
        Cold, on the stroke of midnight,
The tip of one finger touched it! The trigger
    at least was hers!

The tip of one finger touched it; she strove no more
    for the rest!
Up, she stood up to attention, with the barrel beneath
    her breast,
She would not risk their hearing; she would not
    strive again;
For the road lay bare in the moonlight,
        Blank and bare in the moonlight;
And the blood of her veins in the moonlight throbbed
    to her Love's refrain.

Tlot-tlot, tlot-tlot! Had they heard it? The horse-hoofs
    ringing clear—
Tlot-tlot, tlot-tlot, in the distance? Were they deaf that
    they did not hear?
Down the ribbon of moonlight, over the brow of
    the hill,
The highwayman came riding,
        Riding, riding!
The red-coats looked to their priming! She stood up
    straight and still!

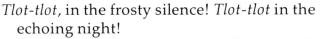

Tlot-tlot, in the frosty silence! *Tlot-tlot* in the
    echoing night!
Nearer he came and nearer! Her face was like a light!
Her eyes grew wide for a moment; she drew one last
    deep breath,
Then her finger moved in the moonlight,
        Her musket shattered the moonlight,
Shattered her breast in the moonlight and warned
    him—with her death.

He turned; he spurred him westward; he did not know
    who stood
Bowed with her head o'er the musket, drenched with
    her own red blood!
Not till the dawn he heard it, and slowly blanched
    to hear
How Bess, the landlord's daughter,
        The landlord's black-eyed daughter,
Had watched for her Love in the moonlight; and died
    in the darkness there.

Back, he spurred like a madman, shrieking a curse to
    the sky,
With the white road smoking behind him, and his
    rapier brandished high!
Blood-red were his spurs i' the golden noon; wine-red
    was his velvet coat;
When they shot him down on the highway,
        Down like a dog on the highway,
And he lay in his blood on the highway, with the
    bunch of lace at his throat.

And still of a winter's night, they say, when the wind
   is in the trees,
When the moon is a ghostly galleon tossed upon
   cloudy seas,
When the road is a ribbon of moonlight over
   the purple moor,
A highwayman comes riding—
      Riding—riding—
A highwayman comes riding, up to the old inn-door.

Over the cobbles he clatters and clangs in the dark
   inn-yard;
And he taps with his whip on the shutters, but all is
   locked and barred:
He whistles a tune to the window, and who should be
   waiting there
But the landlord's black-eyed daughter,
      Bess, the landlord's daughter,
Plaiting a dark red love-knot into her long black hair.

Alfred Noyes

On the Ning Nang Nong

On the Ning Nang Nong
Where the Cows go Bong!
And the Monkeys all say Boo!
There's a Nong Nang Ning
Where the trees go Ping!
And the tea pots Jibber Jabber Joo.
On the Nong Ning Nang
All the mice go Clang!
And you just can't catch 'em when they do!
So it's Ning Nang Nong!
Cows go Bong!
Nong Nang Ning!
Trees go Ping!
Nong Ning Nang!
The mice go Clang!
What a noisy place to belong,
Is the Ning Nang Ning Nang Nong!!

Spike Milligan

Jack Frost

Look out! look out!
Jack Frost is about!
He's after our fingers and toes;
And, all through the night,
The gay little sprite
Is working where nobody knows.

He'll climb each tree,
So nimble is he,
His silvery powder he'll shake;
To windows he'll creep,
And while we're asleep,
Such wonderful pictures he'll make.

Across the grass
He'll merrily pass,
And change all its greenness to white;
Then home he will go,
And laugh, 'Ho! ho! ho!
What fun I have had in the night!'

Cecily Pike

Mrs Moon

Mrs Moon
sitting up in the sky
Little Old Lady
rock-a-bye
with a ball of fading light
and silvery needles
knitting the night.

Roger McGough

If You Should Meet a Crocodile

If you should meet a crocodile,
Don't take a stick and poke him;
Ignore the welcome in his smile,
Be careful not to stroke him.

For as he sleeps upon the Nile,
He thinner gets and thinner;
And whene'er you meet a crocodile
He's ready for his dinner.

Anonymous

Way Down South Where Bananas Grow

Way down south where bananas grow,
A grasshopper stepped on an elephant's toe.
The elephant said, with tears in his eyes,
'Pick on somebody your own size.'

Anonymous

20

Up in a Basket

There was an old woman tossed up in a basket,
　　Seventeen times as high as the moon;
And where she was going, I couldn't but ask it,
　　For in her hand she carried a broom.
Old woman, old woman, old woman, quoth I,
　　O whither, O whither, O whither so high?
To sweep the cobwebs off the sky!
　　Shall I go with you? Aye, by-and-by.

Anonymous

The Hippopotamus

The huge hippopotamus hasn't a hair
on the back of his wrinkly hide;
he carries the bulk of his prominent hulk
rather loosely assembled inside.

The huge hippopotamus lives without care
at a slow philosophical pace,
as he wades in the mud with a thump and a thud
and a permanent grin on his face.

Jack Prelutsky

The Duck

Behold the duck.
It does not cluck.
A cluck it lacks.
It quacks.
It is specially fond
Of a puddle or pond.
When it dines or sups,
It bottoms ups.

Ogden Nash

The Mermaid

I

Who would be
A mermaid fair,
Singing alone,
Combing her hair
Under the sea,
In a golden curl
With a comb of pearl,
On a throne?

II

I would be a mermaid fair;
I would sing to myself the whole of the day.
With a comb of pearl I would comb my hair;
And still as I combed I would sing and say,
'Who is it loves me? who loves not me?'
I would comb my hair till my ringlets would fall,
        Low adown, low adown,
And I should look like a fountain of gold
        Springing alone
        With a shrill inner sound,
        Over the throne
        In the midst of the hall.

The Merman

I

Who would be
A merman bold,
Sitting alone,
Singing alone
Under the sea,
With a crown of gold,
On a throne?

II

I would be a merman bold;
I would sit and sing the whole of the day.
I would fill the sea-halls with a voice of power
But at night I would roam abroad and play
With the mermaids in and out of the rocks,
Dressing their hair with the white sea-flower;
And holding them back by their flowing locks
I would kiss them often under the sea,
And kiss them again till they kissed me
       Laughingly, laughingly;
And then we would wander away, away,
To the pale sea-groves straight and high,
       Chasing each other merrily.

Alfred, Lord Tennyson

Sir Nicketty Nox

Sir Nicketty Nox was an ancient knight,
So old was he that he'd lost his sight.
Blind as a mole, and slim as a fox,
And dry as a stick was Sir Nicketty Nox.

His sword and buckler were old and cracked,
So was his charger and that's a fact.
Thin as a rake from head to hocks,
Was this rickety nag of Sir Nicketty Nox.

A wife he had and daughters three,
And all were as old, as old could be.
They mended the shirts and darned the socks
Of that old Antiquity, Nicketty Nox.

Sir Nicketty Nox would fly in a rage
If anyone tried to guess his age.
He'd mouth and mutter and tear his locks,
This very pernickety Nicketty Nox.

Hugh Chesterman

24

The Balloon Man

He always comes on market days,
   And holds balloons—a lovely bunch—
And in the market square he stays,
   And never seems to think of lunch.

They're red and purple, blue and green,
   And when it is a sunny day
Tho' carts and people get between
   You see them shining far away.

And some are big and some are small,
   All tied together with a string,
And if there is a wind at all
   They tug and tug like anything.

Some day perhaps he'll let them go
   And we shall see them sailing high,
And stand and watch them from below—
   They *would* look pretty in the sky!

Rose Fyleman

The Three Kings

Three Kings came riding from far away,
    Melchior and Gaspar and Baltasar;
Three Wise Men out of the East were they.
And they travelled by night and they slept by day,
    For their guide was a beautiful, wonderful star.

The star was so beautiful, large and clear,
    That all the other stars of the sky
Became a white mist in the atmosphere,
And by this they knew that the coming was near
    Of the Prince foretold in the prophecy.

Three caskets they bore on their saddle-bows,
    Three caskets of gold with golden keys;
Their robes were of crimson silk with rows
Of bells and pomegranates and furbelows,
    Their turbans like blossoming almond-trees.

And so the Three Kings rode into the West,
   Through the dusk of night, over hill and dell,
And sometimes they nodded with beard on breast
And sometimes talked, as they paused to rest,
   With the people they met at some wayside well.

'Of the child that is born,' said Baltasar,
   'Good people, I pray you, tell us the news;
For we in the East have seen his star,
And have ridden fast, and have ridden far,
   To find and worship the King of the Jews.'

And the people answered, 'You ask in vain;
   We know of no king but Herod the Great!'
They thought the Wise Men were men insane,
As they spurred their horses across the plain,
   Like riders in haste, and who cannot wait.

And when they came to Jerusalem,
    Herod the Great, who had heard this thing,
Sent for the Wise Men and questioned them;
And said, 'Go down unto Bethlehem,
    And bring me tidings of this new king.'

So they rode away; and the star stood still,
    The only one in the gray of morn;
Yes, it stopped —it stood still of its own free will,
Right over Bethlehem on the hill,
    The city of David, where Christ was born.

And the Three Kings rode through the gate and
        the guard,
    Through the silent street, till their horses turned
And neighed as they entered the great inn-yard;
But the windows were closed, and the doors
        were barred,
    And only a light in the stable burned.

And there in the scented hay,
    In the air made sweet by the breath of kine,
The little child in the manger lay,
The child, that would be king one day
    Of a kingdom not human but divine.

His mother Mary of Nazareth
   Sat watching beside his place of rest,
Watching the even flow of his breath,
For the joy of life and the terror of death
   Were mingled together in her breast.

They laid their offerings at his feet:
   The gold was their tribute to a King,
The frankincense, with its odour sweet,
Was for the Priest, the Paraclete,
   The myrrh for the body's burying.

And the mother wondered and bowed her head,
   And sat as still as a statue of stone;
Her heart was troubled yet comforted,
Remembering what the Angel had said
   Of an endless reign and of David's throne.

Then the Kings rode out of the city gate,
   With a clatter of hoofs in proud array;
But they went not back to Herod the Great,
For they knew his malice and feared his hate,
   And returned to their homes by another way.

Henry Wadsworth Longfellow

Romance

I saw a ship a-sailing,
A-sailing on the sea;
Her masts were of the shining gold,
Her deck of ivory;
And sails of silk, as soft as milk,
And silvern shrouds had she.

And round about her sailing
The sea was sparkling white,
The waves all clapped their hands and sang
To see so fair a sight;
They kissed her twice, they kissed her thrice,
And murmured with delight.

Then came the gallant captain
And stood upon the deck,
In velvet coat and ruffles white,
Without a spot or speck,
And diamond rings and triple strings
Of pearls about his neck.

And four and twenty sailors
Were round him bowing low,
On every jacket three times three
Gold buttons in a row,
And cutlasses down to their knees;
They made a goodly show.

And then the ship went sailing,
A-sailing o'er the sea;
She dived beneath the setting sun,
But never back came she,
For she found the lands of the golden sands,
Where the pearls and diamonds be.

Gabriel Setoun

Washing

What is all this washing about,
Every day, week in, week out?
From getting up till going to bed,
I'm tired of hearing the same thing said.
Whether I'm dirty or whether I'm not,
Whether the water is cold or hot,
Whether I like or whether I don't,
Whether I will or whether I won't —
'Have you washed your hands, and washed your face?'
I seem to *live* in the washing-place.

Whenever I go for a walk or ride,
As soon as I put my nose inside
The door again, there's some one there
With a sponge and soap, and a lot they care
If I have something better to do,
'Now wash your face and your fingers too.'

Before a meal is ever begun,
And after ever a meal is done,
It's time to turn on the waterspout.
Please, what *is* all this washing about?

John Drinkwater

The Witch

I saw her plucking cowslips,
And marked her where she stood:
She never knew I watched her
While hiding in the wood.

Her skirt was brightest crimson,
And black her steeple hat,
Her broomstick lay beside her—
I'm positive of that.

Her chin was sharp and pointed,
Her eyes were—I don't know—
For, when she turned towards me—
I thought it best—to go!

Percy H. Ilott

The Big Rock Candy Mountains

On a summer's day in the month of May,
A burly bum come a-hiking,
Travelling down that lonesome road
A-looking for his liking.
He was headed for a land that was far away,
Beside them crystal fountains—
'I'll see you all this coming fall
In the Big Rock Candy Mountains.'

In the Big Rock Candy Mountains
You never change your socks,
And little streams of alcohol
Come a-trickling down the rocks.
The box cars are all empty
And the railroad bulls are blind,
There's a lake of stew and whisky, too,
You can paddle all around 'em in a big canoe
In the Big Rock Candy Mountains.

O—the buzzing of the bees in the cigarette trees
Round the soda water fountains,
Where the lemonade springs and the bluebird sings
In the Big Rock Candy Mountains.

In the Big Rock Candy Mountains,
There's a land that's fair and bright,
Where the hand-outs grow on bushes
And you sleep out every night,
Where the box cars are all empty
And the sun shines every day,
O I'm bound to go, where there ain't no snow,
Where the rain don't fall and the wind don't blow
In the Big Rock Candy Mountains.

In the Big Rock Candy Mountains
The jails are made of tin
And you can bust right out again
As soon as they put you in;
The farmers' trees are full of fruit,
The barns are full of hay,
I'm going to stay where you sleep all day,
Where they boiled in oil the inventor of toil
In the Big Rock Candy Mountains.

Anonymous

Sea-Fever

I must down to the seas again, to the lonely sea
    and the sky,
And all I ask is a tall ship and a star to steer her by,
And the wheel's kick and the wind's song and the
    white sail's shaking,
And a grey mist on the sea's face and a grey dawn
    breaking.

I must down to the seas again, for the call of the
    running tide
Is a wild call and a clear call that may not be denied;
And all I ask is a windy day with the white clouds
    flying,
And the flung spray and the blown spume and the
    seagulls crying.

I must down to the seas again to the vagrant gypsy life.
To the gull's way and the whale's way where the
    wind's like a whetted knife;
And all I ask is a merry yarn from a laughing fellow-
    rover,
And quiet sleep and a sweet dream when the long
    trick's over.

John Masefield

Who Has Seen the Wind?

Who has seen the wind?
Neither I nor you:
But when the leaves hang trembling,
The wind is passing through.

Who has seen the wind?
Neither you nor I:
But when the trees bow down their heads,
The wind is passing by.

Christina Rossetti

The Serpent

There was a Serpent who had to sing.
There was. There was.
He simply gave up Serpenting.
Because. Because.

He didn't like his Kind of Life;
He couldn't find a proper Wife;
He was a Serpent with a soul;
He got no Pleasure down his Hole.
And so, of course, he had to Sing,
And Sing he did, like Anything!
The Birds, they were, they were Astounded;
And various Measures Propounded
To stop the Serpent's Awful Racket:
They bought a Drum. He wouldn't Whack it.
They sent,—you always send,—to Cuba
And got a Most Commodious Tuba;
They got a Horn, they got a Flute,
But Nothing would suit.
He said, 'Look, Birds, all this is futile:
I do *not* like to Bang or Tootle.'
And then he cut loose with a Horrible Note
That practically split the Top of his Throat.
'You see,' he said, with a Serpent's Leer,
'I'm Serious about my Singing Career!'
And the Woods Resounded with many a Shriek
As the Birds flew off to the End of Next Week.

Theodore Roethke

He Was a Rat

He was a rat, and she was a rat,
    And down in one hole they did dwell,
And both were as black as a witch's cat,
    And they loved each other well.

He had a tail, and she had a tail,
    Both long and curling and fine;
And each said, 'Yours is the finest tail
    In the world, excepting mine.'

He smelt the cheese, and she smelt the cheese,
    And they both pronounced it good;
And both remarked it would greatly add
    To the charms of their daily food.

So he ventured out, and she ventured out,
    And I saw them go with pain;
But what befell them I never can tell
    For they never came back again.

Anonymous

The Lobster Quadrille

'Will you walk a little faster?'
Said a whiting to a snail,
'There's a porpoise close behind us,
And he's treading on my tail.
See how eagerly the lobsters
And the turtles all advance!
They are waiting on the shingle—
Will you come and join the dance?
    Will you, won't you, will you, won't you,
    Will you join the dance?
    Will you, won't you, will you, won't you,
    Won't you join the dance?

'You can really have no notion
How delightful it will be,
When they take us up and throw us,
With the lobsters, out to sea!'
But the snail replied, 'Too far, too far!'
And gave a look askance,
Said he thanked the whiting kindly,
But he would not join the dance,
    Would not, could not, would not, could not,
    Would not join the dance,
    Would not, could not, would not, could not,
    Could not join the dance.

'What matters it how far we go?'
His scaly friend replied.
'There is another shore, you know,
Upon the other side.
The further off from England
The nearer is to France—
Then turn not pale, beloved snail,
But come and join the dance.
    Will you, won't you, will you, won't you,
    Will you join the dance?
    Will you, won't you, will you, won't you,
    Won't you join the dance?'

Lewis Carroll

The Dustman

When the shades of night are falling, and the sun
    goes down,
O! the Dustman comes a-creeping in from Shut-eye Town.
And he throws dust in the eyes of all the babies that
    he meets,
No matter where he finds them, in the house
    or in the streets.
Then the babies' eyes grow heavy and the lids drop down,
When the Dustman comes a-creeping in from
    Shut-eye Town.

When mother lights the lamp and draws the curtains down,
O! the Dustman comes a-creeping in from Shut-eye Town,
And the babies think the Dustman is as mean as he can be,
For he shuts their eyes at nightfall, just when they
    want to see.
But their little limbs are weary, for all they fret
    and frown,
When the Dustman comes a-creeping in from
    Shut-eye Town.

Anonymous

The Table and the Chair

Said the Table to the Chair,
'You can hardly be aware
How I suffer from the heat
And from chilblains on my feet.
If we took a little walk,
We might have a little talk;
Pray let us take the air,'
Said the Table to the Chair.

Said the Chair unto the Table,
'Now, you know we are not able:
How foolishly you talk,
When you know we cannot walk!'
Said the Table with a sigh,
'It can do no harm to try.
I've as many legs as you;
Why can't we walk on two?'

So they both went slowly down,
And walked about the town
With a cheerful bumpy sound
As they toddled round and round;
And everybody cried,
As they hastened to their side,
'See! the Table and the Chair
Have come out to take the air!'

But in going down an alley
To a castle in a valley,
They completely lost their way,
And wandered all the day;
Till, to see them safely back,
They paid a Ducky-quack,
And a Beetle, and a Mouse,
Who took them to their house.

Then they whispered to each other,
'O delightful little brother,
What a lovely walk we've taken!
Let us dine on beans and bacon.'
So the Ducky and the leetle
Browny-Mousy *and* the Beetle
Dined and danced upon their heads
Till they toddled to their beds.

Edward Lear

Fairies

There are fairies at the bottom of our garden!
    It's not so very, very far away;
You pass the gardener's shed and you just keep
    straight ahead—
    I do so hope they've really come to stay.
There's a little wood, with moss in it and beetles,
    And a little stream that quietly runs through;
You wouldn't think they'd dare to come merry-making
    there—
        Well, they do.

There are fairies at the bottom of our garden!
    They often have a dance on summer nights;
The butterflies and bees make a lovely little breeze,
    And the rabbits stand about and hold the lights.
Did you know that they could sit upon the moonbeams
    And pick a little star to make a fan,
And dance away up there in the middle of the air?
        Well, they can.

There are fairies at the bottom of our garden!
　　You cannot think how beautiful they are;
They all stand up and sing when the Fairy Queen and King
　　Come gently floating down upon their car.
The King is very proud and *very* handsome;
　　The Queen—now can you guess who that could be
(She's a little girl all day, but at night she steals away)?
　　　　Well—it's Me!

Rose Fyleman

Father William

'You are old, Father William,' the young man said,
  'And your hair has become very white;
And yet you incessantly stand on your head—
  Do you think, at your age, it is right?'

'In my youth,' Father William replied to his son,
  'I feared it might injure the brain;
But now that I'm perfectly sure I have none,
  Why, I do it again and again.'

'You are old,' said the youth, 'as I mentioned before,
  And have grown most uncommonly fat;
Yet you turned a back somersault in at the door—
  Pray, what is the reason of that?'

'In my youth,' said the sage, as he shook his grey locks,
  'I kept all my limbs very supple.
By the use of this ointment—one shilling the box—
  Allow me to sell you a couple?'

'You are old,' said the youth, 'and your jaws are too weak
    For anything tougher than suet;
Yet you finished the goose, with the bones and the beak—
    Pray, how did you manage to do it?'

'In my youth,' said his father, 'I took to the law,
    And argued each case with my wife;
And the muscular strength which it gave to my jaw,
    Has lasted the rest of my life.'

'You are old,' said the youth, 'one would hardly suppose
    That your eye was as steady as ever;
Yet you balanced an eel on the end of your nose—
    What made you so awfully clever?'

'I have answered three questions, and that is enough,'
    Said his father. 'Don't give yourself airs!
Do you think I can listen all day to such stuff!
    Be off, or I'll kick you downstairs!'

Lewis Carroll

Cat!

Cat!
Scat!
Atter her, atter her,
Sleeky flatterer,
Spitfire chatterer,
Scatter her, scatter her
  Off her mat!
  Wuff!
  Wuff!
  Treat her rough!
Git her, git her,
Whiskery spitter!
Catch her, catch her,
Green-eyed scratcher!
  Slathery
  Slithery
  Hisser,
  Don't miss her!
Run till you're dithery,
  Hithery
  Thithery
  Pfitts! Pfitts!
  How she spits!
  Spitch! Spatch!
  Can't she scratch!
Scritching the bark
Of the sycamore-tree,
She's reached her ark
And's hissing at me
  Pfitts! Pfitts!
  Wuff! Wuff!
    Scat,
    Cat!
    That's
    That!

Eleanor Farjeon

The Frog and the Bird

By a quiet little stream on an old mossy log,
Looking very forlorn, sat a little green frog;
He'd a sleek speckled back, and two bright yellow eyes,
And when dining, selected the choicest of flies.

The sun was so hot he scarce opened his eyes,
Far too lazy to stir, let alone watch for flies,
He was nodding, and nodding, and almost asleep,
When a voice in the branches chirped: 'Froggie, cheep,
    cheep!'

'You'd better take care,' piped the bird to the frog,
'In the water you'll be if you fall off that log.
Can't you see that the streamlet is up to the brim?'
Croaked the froggie: 'What odds! You forget I can swim!'

Then the froggie looked up at the bird perched so high
On a bough that to him seemed to reach to the sky;
So he croaked to the bird: 'If you fall, you will die!'
Chirped the birdie: 'What odds! You forget I can fly!'

Vera Hessey

Winter the Huntsman

Through his iron glades
Rides Winter the Huntsman.
All colour fades
As his horn is heard sighing.

Far through the forest
His wild hooves crash and thunder
Till many a mighty branch
Is torn asunder.

As the red reynard creeps
To his hole near the river,
The copper leaves fall
And the bare trees shiver.

As night creeps from the ground,
Hides each tree from its brother,
And each dying sound
Reveals yet another.

Is it Winter the Huntsman
Who gallops through his iron glades,
Cracking his cruel whip
To the gathering shades?

Osbert Sitwell

The Traveller

Old man, old man, sitting on the stile,
Your boots are worn, your clothes are torn,
　Tell us why you smile.

Children, children, what silly things you are!
My boots are worn and my clothes are torn
　Because I've walked so far.

Old man, old man, where have you walked from?
Your legs are bent, your breath is spent—
　Which way did you come?

Children, children, when you're old and lame,
When your legs are bent and your breath is spent
　You'll know the way I came.

Old man, old man, have you far to go
Without a friend to your journey's end,
　And why are you so slow?

Children, children, I do the best I may:
I meet a friend at my journey's end
　With whom you'll meet some day.

Old man, old man, sitting on the stile,
How do you know which way to go,
　And why is it you smile?

Children, children, butter should be spread,
Floors should be swept and promises kept—
　And you should be in bed!

Raymond Wilson

Nothing

He thought he heard
A footstep on the stair,
'It's nothing,' he said to himself,
'Nothing is there.'
He thought then he heard
A snuffling in the hall,
'It's nothing,' he said again,
'Nothing at all.'
But he didn't open the door
In case he found nothing
Standing there,
On foot or tentacle or paw.
Timidly quiet he kept to his seat
While nothing stalked the house
On great big feet.
It was strange though
And he'd noticed this
When on his own before,
Nothing stalked throughout the house
But never through his door.
The answer he thought,
Was very plain. It was because there was
nothing there—
Again!

Julie Holder

The Hag

The Hag is astride,
This night for to ride;
The Devil and she together:
Through thick, and through thin,
Now out, and then in,
Though ne'er so foul be the weather.

A Thorn or a Burr
She takes for a Spur:
With a lash of a Bramble she rides now,
Through Brakes and through Briars,
O'er Ditches, and Mires,
She follows the Spirit that guides now.

No Beast, for his food,
Dares now range the wood;
But hush't in his lair he lies lurking:
While mischiefs, by these,
On Land and on Seas,
At noon of Night are a working.

The storm will arise,
And trouble the skies;
This night, and more for the wonder,
The ghost from the Tomb
Affrighted shall come,
Called out by the clap of the Thunder.

Robert Herrick

The Skippery Boo

I went to bring,
From the rippling spring,
One morning dry and damp,
A brimming pail
Of Adam's ale
For use about the camp;
My happy frame
Did well proclaim
A cheerful bent of mind,
And I hummed a song,
As I loped along,
Of the most enchanting kind.
But my heart stood still,
As I turned the hill,
And the spring came to my view,
For drinking there
Of the potion rare,
Was the terrible Skippery Boo.

He drank his fill
From the flowing rill,
And shook his mighty mane,
Then with his jaws
And his hairy paws,
He ripped a tree in twain.
With fear and dread
To camp I sped,
For my trusty .30 bore,
Then turned about
With daring shout,
And sought the spring once more;
But though my feet
With speed were fleet,
As o'er the glade I flew,
No sign was there
On earth, in air,
Of the slippery Skippery Boo.

To left and right
I strained my sight,
To find where he had gone,
Among the pines
I sought for signs,
But found not a single one.
To East and West
I turned my quest,
But all to no avail,
No trace I found
On gorse or ground,
Of his departing trail.
And then aloft
My gaze I doffed,
And there in the hazy blue,
On the topmost spine
Of the tallest pine,
Hung the fabulous Skippery Boo.

Oh, the Skippery Boo
Is a fanciful zoo:
A mermaid and a bat,
A grizzly hare
And a webfoot bear,
A goof and a bumble-cat.
He can fell an oak
With a single stroke,
Or shatter a mountain side,
Then lightly rise
To the azure skies,
And light as a zephyr ride.
My heart he fills
With terror's chills,
Oh, don't know what I'd do,
If some dark night,
In broad daylight,
I should meet a Skippery Boo.

A poison flows
From his warty toes,
And the grass where he shall tread,
Shall wilt and fade
At evening's shade,
And tomorrow shall be dead.
And who shall walk
Where he shall stalk,
O'er valley, hill or plain,
Shall die, 'tis said,
Of illness dread,
And a terrible dark-green pain.
So as you wade
This vale of shade,
And jog life's journey through,
At day, at night,
Be it dark or light,
Watch out for the Skippery Boo.

Earl L. Newton

The Moon

The moon has a face like the clock in the hall;
She shines on thieves on the garden wall,
On streets and fields and harbour quays,
And birdies asleep in the forks of the trees.

The squalling cat and the squeaking mouse,
The howling dog by the door of the house,
The bat that lies in bed at noon,
All love to be out by the light of the moon.

But all of the things that belong to the day
Cuddle to sleep to be out of her way;
And flowers and children close their eyes
Till up in the morning the sun shall rise.

Robert Louis Stevenson

The Witches' Call

Come, witches, come, on your hithering brooms!
The moorland is dark and still
Over the church and the churchyard tombs
To the oakwood under the hill.

Come through the mist and the wandering cloud,
Fly with the crescent moon;
Come where the witches and warlocks crowd,
Come soon . . . soon!

Leave your room with its shadowy cat,
Your cauldron over the hearth;
Seize your cloak and pointed hat,
Come by the witches' path.
Float from the earth like a rising bird,
Stream through the darkening air,
Come at the sound of our secret word,
Come to the witches' lair!

Clive Sansom

Past, present, future

Tell me, tell me, smiling child,
What the past is like to thee?
'An Autumn evening soft and mild
With a wind that sighs mournfully.'

Tell me, what is the present hour?
'A green and flowery spray
Where a young bird sits gathering its power
To mount and fly away.'

And what is the future, happy one?
'A sea beneath a cloudless sun;
A mighty, glorious, dazzling sea
Stretching into infinity.'

Emily Brontë

Where Lies the Land?

Where lies the land to which the ship would go?
Far, far ahead, is all her seamen know.
And where the land she travels from? Away,
Far, far behind, is all that they can say.

On sunny morns upon the deck's smooth face,
Linked arm in arm, how pleasant here to pace;
Or, o'er the stern reclining, watch below
The foaming wake far widening as we go.

On stormy nights when wild north-westers rave,
How proud a thing to fight with wind and wave!
The dripping sailor on the reeling mast
Exults to bear, and scorns to wish it past.

Where lies the land to which the ship would go?
Far, far ahead, is all her seamen know.
And where the land she travels from? Away,
Far, far behind, is all that they can say.

A. H. Clough

The Fairies

Up the airy mountain,
  Down the rushy glen,
We daren't go a-hunting
  For fear of little men;
Wee folk, good folk,
  Trooping all together;
Green jacket, red cap,
  And white owl's feather.

Down along the rocky shore
  Some make their home—
They live on crispy pancakes
  Of yellow tide-foam;
Some in the reeds
  Of the black mountain lake,
With frogs for their watch-dogs,
  All night awake.

High on the hill-top
  The old King sits;
He is now so old and grey
  He's nigh lost his wits.
With a bridge of white mist
  Columbkill he crosses,
On his stately journeys
  From Slieveleague to Rosses;
Or going up with music
  On cold starry nights,
To sup with the Queen
  Of the gay Northern Lights.

They stole little Bridget
  For seven years long;
When she came down again
  Her friends were all gone.
They took her lightly back,
  Between the night and morrow,
They thought that she was fast asleep,
  But she was dead with sorrow.
They have kept her ever since
  Deep within the lake,
On a bed of flag-leaves,
  Watching till she wake.

By the craggy hill-side,
  Through the mosses bare,
They have planted thorn-trees
  For pleasure here and there.
Is any man so daring
  As dig them up in spite,
He shall find their sharpest thorns
  In his bed at night.

Up the airy mountain,
  Down the rushy glen,
We daren't go a-hunting
  For fear of little men;
Wee folk, good folk,
  Trooping all together;
Green jacket, red cap,
  And white owl's feather!

William Allingham

The Butterfly's Ball

Come take up your hats, and away let us haste
To the butterfly's ball and the grasshopper's feast;
The trumpeter gadfly has summoned the crew,
And the revels are now only waiting for you.
On the smooth shaven grass, by the side of the wood,
Beneath a broad oak that for ages has stood,
See the children of earth, and the tenants of air,
For an evening's amusement together repair.

And there came the beetle so blind and so black,
Who carried the emmet, his friend, on his back;
And there was the gnat, and the dragon-fly too,
With all their relations, green, orange, and blue.

And there came the moth in his plumage of down,
And the hornet in jacket of yellow and brown,
Who with him the wasp his companion did bring,
But they promised that evening to lay by their sting.

And the sly little dormouse crept out of his hole,
And led to the feast his blind brother the mole,
And the snail, with his horns peeping out from
   his shell,
Came from a great distance—the length of an ell.

A mushroom their table, and on it was laid
A water-dock leaf, which a table-cloth made;
The viands were various, to each of their taste,
And the bee brought his honey to crown the repast.

There, close on his haunches, so solemn and wise,
The frog from a corner looked up to the skies;
And the squirrel, well pleased such diversions to see,
Sat cracking his nuts overhead in a tree.

Then out came the spider, with fingers so fine,
To show his dexterity on the tight line;
From one branch to another his cobwebs he slung,
Then, quick as an arrow, he darted along.

But just in the middle, oh! shocking to tell!
From his rope in an instant poor Harlequin fell;
Yet he touched not the ground, but with talons
    outspread,
Hung suspended in air at the end of a thread.

Then the grasshopper came with a jerk and a spring,
Very long was his leg, though but short was his wing;
He took but three leaps, and was soon out of sight,
Then chirped his own praises the rest of the night.

With step so majestic, the snail did advance,
And promised the gazers a minuet to dance;
But they all laughed so loud that he pulled in his head,
And went in his own little chamber to bed.

Then as evening gave way to the shadows of night
Their watchman, the glowworm, came out with
    his light;
Then home let us hasten while yet we can see,
For no watchman is waiting for you and for me.

William Roscoe

Meg Merrilees

Old Meg she was a Gipsy,
   And liv'd upon the Moors:
Her bed it was the brown heath turf,
   And her house was out of doors.

Her apples were swart blackberries,
   Her currants pods o' broom;
Her wine was dew o' the wild white rose,
   Her book a churchyard tomb.

Her Brothers were the craggy hills,
   Her Sisters larchen trees—
Alone with her great family
   She liv'd as she did please.

No breakfast had she many a morn,
   No dinner many a noon,
And 'stead of supper she would stare
   Full hard against the Moon.

But every morn of woodbine fresh
   She made her garlanding,
And every night the dark glen Yew
   She wove, and she would sing.

And with her fingers old and brown,
   She plaited Mats o' Rushes,
And gave them to the Cottagers
   She met among the Bushes.

Old Meg was brave as Margaret Queen
   And tall as Amazon:
An old red blanket cloak she wore;
   A chip hat had she on.
God rest her aged bones somewhere—
   She died full long agone!

John Keats

My Shadow

I have a little shadow that goes in and out with me,
And what can be the use of him is more than I can see.
He is very, very like me from the heels up to the head;
And I see him jump before me, when I jump into my bed.

The funniest thing about him is the way he likes to grow—
Not at all like proper children, which is always very slow:
For he sometimes shoots up taller like an india-rubber ball,
And he sometimes gets so little that there's none of him
    at all.

He hasn't got a notion of how children ought to play,
And can only make a fool of me in every sort of way.
He stays so close beside me, he's a coward you can see;
I'd think shame to stick to nursie as that shadow sticks
    to me!

One morning, very early, before the sun was up,
I rose and found the shining dew on every buttercup;
But my lazy little shadow, like an arrant sleepy-head,
Had stayed at home behind me and was fast asleep
    in bed.

Robert Louis Stevenson

Johnny Crow's Garden

Johnny Crow
Would dig and sow
Till he made a little Garden.

And the Lion
Had a green and yellow Tie on
In Johnny Crow's Garden.

And the Rat
Wore a Feather in his Hat
But the Bear
Had nothing to wear
In Johnny Crow's Garden.

So the Ape
Took his Measure with a Tape
In Johnny Crow's Garden.

Then the Crane
Was caught in the Rain
In Johnny Crow's Garden.

And the Beaver
Was afraid he had a Fever
But the Goat
Said:
'It's nothing but his Throat'
In Johnny Crow's Garden.

And the Pig
Danced a Jig
In Johnny Crow's Garden.

Then the Stork
Gave a Philosophic Talk
Till the Hippopotami
Said: 'Ask no further "What am I?"'
While the Elephant
Said something quite irrelevant
In Johnny Crow's Garden.

And the Goose—
Well,
The Goose *was* a Goose
In Johnny Crow's Garden.

And the Mouse
Built himself a little House
Where the Cat
Sat down beside the Mat
In Johnny Crow's Garden.

And the Whale
Told a very long Tale
In Johnny Crow's Garden.

And the Owl
Was a funny old Fowl
And the Fox
Put them all in the Stocks
In Johnny Crow's Garden.

But Johnny Crow
He let them go
And they all sat down
To their dinner in a row
In Johnny Crow's Garden!

L. Leslie Brooke

71

Silver

Slowly, silently, now the moon
Walks the night in her silver shoon;
This way, and that, she peers, and sees
Silver fruit upon silver trees;
One by one the casements catch
Her beams beneath the silvery thatch;
Couched in his kennel, like a log,
With paws of silver sleeps the dog;
From their shadowy cote the white breasts peep
Of doves in a silver-feathered sleep;
A harvest mouse goes scampering by,
With silver claws, and silver eye;
And moveless fish in the water gleam,
By silver reeds in a silver stream.

Walter de la Mare

The Wind

I saw you toss the kites on high
And blow the birds about the sky;
And all around I heard you pass,
Like ladies' skirts across the grass—
    O wind, a-blowing all day long,
    O wind, that sings so loud a song!

I saw the different things you did,
But always you yourself you hid.
I felt you push, I heard you call,
I could not see yourself at all—
    O wind, a-blowing all day long,
    O wind, that sings so loud a song!

O you that are so strong and cold,
O blower, are you young or old?
Are you a beast of field and tree,
Or just a stronger child than me?
    O wind, a-blowing all day long,
    O wind, that sings so loud a song!

Robert Louis Stevenson

The Fly-Away Horse

Oh, a wonderful horse is the Fly-Away Horse—
    Perhaps you have seen him before;
Perhaps, while you slept, his shadow has swept
    Through the moonlight that floats on the floor.
For it's only at night, when the stars twinkle bright,
    That the Fly-Away Horse, with a neigh
And a pull at his rein and a toss of his mane,
      Is up on his heels and away!
        The Moon in the sky,
        As he gallopeth by,
      Cries: 'Oh! what a marvellous sight!'
        And the Stars in dismay
        Hide their faces away
In the lap of old Grandmother Night.

It is yonder, out yonder, the Fly-Away Horse
    Speedeth ever and ever away—
Over meadows and lanes, over mountains and plains,
    Over streamlets that sing at their play;
And over the sea like a ghost sweepeth he,
    While the ships they go sailing below,
And he speedeth so fast that the men at the mast
    Adjudge him some portent of woe.
      'What ho, there!' they cry,
      As he flourishes by
With a whisk of his beautiful tail;
      And the fish in the sea
      Are as scared as can be,
From the nautilus up to the whale!

And the Fly-Away Horse seeks those far-away lands
    You little folk dream of at night—
Where candy-trees grow, and honey-brooks flow,
    And corn-fields with popcorn are white;
And the beasts in the wood are ever so good
    To children who visit them there—
What glory astride of a lion to ride,
    Or to wrestle around with a bear!
      The monkeys, they say:
       'Come on, let us play,'
    And they frisk in the coconut-trees:
      While the parrots, that cling
      To the peanut-vines, sing
Or converse with comparative ease!

Off! scamper to bed—you shall ride him tonight!
    For, as soon as you've fallen asleep,
With jubilant neigh he shall bear you away
    Over forest and hillside and deep!
But tell us, my dear, all you see and you hear
    In those beautiful lands over there,
Where the Fly-Away Horse wings his far-away course
    With the wee one consigned to his care.
      Then Grandma will cry
      In amazement: 'Oh, my!'
    And she'll think it could never be so.
      And only we two
      Shall know it is true—
You and I, little precious! shall know!

Eugene Field

Bedtime

The evening is coming,
The sun sinks to rest;
The rooks are all flying
Straight home to the nest.
'Caw!' says the rook, as he flies overhead;
'It's time little people were going to bed!'

The flowers are closing;
The daisy's asleep;
The primrose is buried
In slumber so deep.
Shut up for the night is the pimpernel red;
It's time little people were going to bed!

The butterfly, drowsy,
Has folded its wing;
The bees are returning;
No more the birds sing—
Their labour is over, their nestlings are fed;
It's time little people were going to bed!

Here comes the pony—
His work is all done;
Down through the meadow
He takes a good run;
Up go his heels, and down goes his head;
It's time little people were going to bed!

Good-night, little people,
Good-night, and good-night;
Sweet dreams to your eyelids
Till dawning of light;
The evening has come, there's no more to be said;
It's time little people were going to bed!

Thomas Hood

My Heart's in the Highlands

My heart's in the Highlands, my heart is not here;
My heart's in the Highlands a-chasing the deer;
Chasing the wild deer, and following the roe,
My heart's in the Highlands wherever I go.
Farewell to the Highlands, farewell to the North,
The birth-place of valour, the country of worth;
Wherever I wander, wherever I rove,
The hills of the Highlands for ever I love.

Farewell to the mountains, high covered with snow;
Farewell to the straths and green valleys below;
Farewell to the forests and wild-hanging woods;
Farewell to the torrents and loud-pouring floods.
My heart's in the Highlands, my heart is not here;
My heart's in the Highlands a-chasing the deer;
Chasing the wild deer, and following the roe,
My heart's in the Highlands, wherever I go.

Robert Burns

Little Trotty Wagtail

Little trotty wagtail, he went in the rain,
And twittering, tottering sideways he ne'er got straight
   again.
He stooped to get a worm, and looked up to get a fly,
And then he flew away ere his feathers they were dry.

Little trotty wagtail, he waddled in the mud,
And he left his little footmarks, trample where
   he would.
He waddled in the water-pudge, and waggle went
   his tail,
And chirrup up his wings to dry upon the garden rail.

Little trotty wagtail, you nimble all about,
And in the dimpling water-pudge you waddle
   in and out;
Your home is nigh at hand, and in the warm pig-stye,
So little Master Wagtail, I'll bid you a good-bye.

John Clare

Calico Pie

Calico Pie,
  The little Birds fly
Down to the calico tree,
  Their wings were blue,
  And they sang 'Tilly-loo!'
Till away they flew—
    And they never came back to me!
      They never came back!
      They never came back!
    They never came back to me!

Calico Ban,
  The little Mice ran,
To be ready in time for tea,
  Flippity flup,
  They drank it all up,
And danced in the cup,—
    But they never came back to me!
      They never came back!
      They never came back!
    They never came back to me!

Calico Jam,
  The little Fish swam,
Over the syllabub sea,
  He took off his hat,
  To the Sole and the Sprat,
And the Willeby-wat,—
    But he never came back to me!
      He never came back!
      He never came back!
    He never came back to me!

Calico Drum,
  The Grasshoppers come,
The Butterfly, Beetle, and Bee,
  Over the ground,
  Around and around,
With a hop and a bound,—
    But they never came back!
      They never came back!
      They never came back!
    They never came back to me!

Edward Lear

Lochinvar

Oh, young Lochinvar is come out of the West,—
Through all the wide Border his steed was the best,
And save his good broadsword he weapons had none,—
He rode all unarm'd and he rode all alone.
So faithful in love, and so dauntless in war,
There never was knight like the young Lochinvar.

He stay'd not for brake, and he stopp'd not for stone,
He swam the Eske river where ford there was none,
But ere he alighted at Netherby gate,
The bride had consented, the gallant came late;
For a laggard in love and a dastard in war
Was to wed the fair Ellen of brave Lochinvar.

So boldly he enter'd the Netherby hall,
'Mong bridesmen and kinsmen and brothers and all.
Then spoke the bride's father, his hand on his sword
(For the poor craven bridegroom said never a word),
'Oh, come ye in peace here, or come ye in war,
Or to dance at our bridal, young Lord Lochinvar?'

'I long woo'd your daughter—my suit you denied;
Love swells like the Solway, but ebbs like its tide;
And now am I come, with this lost love of mine
To lead but one measure, drink one cup of wine.
There are maidens in Scotland more lovely, by far,
That would gladly be bride to the young Lochinvar.'

The bride kissed the goblet, the knight took it up,
He quaff'd off the wine and he threw down the cup.
She look'd down to blush, and she look'd up to sigh,
With a smile on her lips and a tear in her eye.
He took her soft hand ere her mother could bar:
'Now tread we a measure,' said young Lochinvar.

So stately his form, and so lovely her face,
That never a hall such a galliard did grace,
While her mother did fret, and her father did fume,
And the bridegroom stood dangling his bonnet and
  plume,
And the bridesmaids whisper'd, 'Twere better by far
To have match'd our fair cousin with young Lochinvar.'

One touch to her hand, and one word in her ear,
When they reach'd the hall-door, and the charger
   stood near;
So light to the croup the fair lady he swung,
So light to the saddle before her he sprung!
'She is won! we are gone, over bank, bush, and scaur;
They'll have fleet steeds that follow,' quoth young
   Lochinvar.

There was mounting 'mong Graemes of the Netherby clan;
Forsters, Fenwicks, and Musgraves, they rode and they ran;
There was racing and chasing on Cannobie Lee,
But the lost bride of Netherby ne'er did they see.
So daring in love, and so dauntless in war,
Have ye e'er heard of gallant like young Lochinvar?

Sir Walter Scott

The Tiger

Tiger! Tiger! burning bright
In the forests of the night,
What immortal hand or eye
Could frame thy fearful symmetry?

In what distant deeps or skies
Burnt the fire of thine eyes?
On what wings dare he aspire?
What the hand dare seize the fire?

And what shoulder, and what art
Could twist the sinews of thy heart?
And, when thy heart began to beat,
What dread hand forged thy dread feet?

What the hammer? what the chain?
In what furnace was thy brain?
What the anvil? what dread grasp
Dare its deadly terrors clasp?

When the stars threw down their spears,
And watered heaven with their tears,
Did he smile his work to see?
Did he who made the Lamb make thee?

Tiger! Tiger! burning bright
In the forests of the night,
What immortal hand or eye
Dare frame thy fearful symmetry?

William Blake

The Night will Never Stay

The night will never stay,
The night will still go by,
Though with a million stars
You pin it to the sky;
Though you bind it with the blowing wind
And buckle it with the moon,
The night will slip away
Like sorrow or a tune.

Eleanor Farjeon

From a Railway Carriage

Faster than fairies, faster than witches,
Bridges and houses, hedges and ditches;
And charging along like troops in a battle,
All through the meadows the horses and cattle:
All of the sights of the hill and the plain
Fly as thick as driving rain;
And ever again, in the wink of an eye,
Painted stations whistle by.

Here is a child who clambers and scrambles,
All by himself and gathering brambles;
Here is a tramp who stands and gazes;
And there is the green for stringing the daisies!
Here is a cart run away in the road
Lumping along with man and load;
And here is a mill, and there is a river:
Each a glimpse and gone for ever!

Robert Louis Stevenson

My Dog, Spot

I have a white dog
Whose name is Spot,
And he's sometimes white
And he's sometimes not.
But whether he's white
Or whether he's not,
There's a patch on his ear
That makes him Spot.

He has a tongue
That is long and pink,
And he lolls it out
When he wants to think.
He seems to think most
When the weather is hot
He's a wise sort of dog,
Is my dog, Spot.

He likes a bone
And he likes a ball,
But he doesn't care
For a cat at all.
He waggles his tail
And he knows what's what,
So I'm glad that he's my dog,
My dog, Spot.

Rodney Bennett

I Wandered Lonely as a Cloud

I wandered lonely as a cloud
That floats on high o'er vales and hills,
When all at once I saw a crowd,
A host, of golden daffodils;
Beside the lake, beneath the trees,
Fluttering and dancing in the breeze.

Continuous as the stars that shine
And twinkle on the milky way,
They stretched in never-ending line
Along the margin of a bay:
Ten thousand saw I at a glance,
Tossing their heads in sprightly dance.

The waves beside them danced; but they
Out-did the sparkling waves in glee:
A poet could not but be gay,
In such a jocund company:
I gazed—and gazed—but little thought
What wealth the show to me had brought:

For oft, when on my couch I lie
In vacant or in pensive mood,
They flash upon that inward eye
Which is the bliss of solitude;
And then my heart with pleasure fills,
And dances with the daffodils.

William Wordsworth

The Owl

When cats run home and light is come,
   And dew is cold upon the ground,
And the far-off stream is dumb,
   And the whirring sail goes round,
   And the whirring sail goes round;
     Alone and warming his five wits,
     The white owl in the belfry sits.

When merry milkmaids click the latch,
   And rarely smells the new-mown hay,
And the cock hath sung beneath the thatch
   Twice or thrice his roundelay,
   Twice or thrice his roundelay;
     Alone and warming his five wits,
     The white owl in the belfry sits.

Alfred, Lord Tennyson

The Wind

Some one tapped at the window pane
  A little while ago.
Some one runs around the house,
  And whistles loud and low.
Some one shakes the garden gate,
  And climbs the garden wall.
Yet when I say:—'Who's that out there?'
  It's nobody at all.
He's calling down the chimney now,
  With quite a noisy roar;
He's piping through the key-hole,
  And he's knocking on the door.
'Come in! Come in!' But no one comes.
  I peep into the hall,
And though I feel a puff of wind,
  There's no one there at all.

John Lea

The Cowboy's Lament

As I walked out in the streets of Laredo,
As I walked out in Laredo one day,
I spied a poor cowboy wrapped up in white linen,
Wrapped up in white linen as cold as the clay.

Oh beat the drum slowly and play the fife lowly,
Play the Dead March as you carry me along;
Take me to the green valley, there lay the sod o'er me,
For I'm a young cowboy and I know I've done wrong.

I see by your outfit that you are a cowboy—
These words he did say as I boldly stepped by.
Come sit down beside me and hear my sad story,
I am shot in the breast and I know I must die.

Let sixteen gamblers come handle my coffin,
Let sixteen cowboys come sing me a song.
Take me to the graveyard and lay the sod o'er me,
For I'm a poor cowboy and I know I've done wrong.

My friends and relations they live in the Nation,
They know not where their boy has gone.
I first came to Texas and hired to a ranchman.
Oh I'm a young cowboy and I know I've done wrong.

It was once in the saddle I used to go dashing,
It was once in the saddle I used to go gay.
First to the dram-house and then to the card-house,
Got shot in the breast and I am dying today.

Get six jolly cowboys to carry my coffin,
Get six pretty maidens to bear up my pall.
Put bunches of roses all over my coffin,
Put roses to deaden the sods as they fall.

Then swing your rope slowly and rattle your spurs
    lowly,
And give a wild whoop as you carry me along,
And in the grave throw me and roll the sod o'er me,
For I'm a young cowboy and I know I've done wrong.

Oh bury beside me my knife and six-shooter,
My spurs on my heel, as you sing me a song,
And over my coffin put a bottle of brandy
That the cowboys may drink as they carry me along.

Go bring me a cup, a cup of cold water
To cool my parched lips, the cowboy then said;
Before I returned his soul had departed,
And gone to the round-up, the cowboy was dead.

We beat the drum slowly and played the fife lowly,
And bitterly wept as we bore him along;
For we all loved our comrade, so brave, young,
    and handsome,
We all loved our comrade although he'd done wrong.

Anonymous

94

Two Witches

There was a witch
The witch had an itch
The itch was so itchy it
Gave her a twitch.

Another witch
Admired the twitch
So she started twitching
Though she had no itch.

Now both of them twitch
So it's hard to tell which
Witch has the itch and
Which witch has the twitch.

Alexander Resnikoff

The Song of Mr. Toad

The world has held great Heroes,
  As history books have showed;
But never a name to go down to fame
  Compared with that of Toad!

The clever men at Oxford
  Know all that there is to be knowed,
But they none of them know one half as much
  As intelligent Mr. Toad!

The animals sat in the Ark and cried,
  Their tears in torrents flowed.
Who was it said, 'There's land ahead'?
  Encouraging Mr. Toad!

The Army all saluted
  As they marched along the road.
Was it the King? Or Kitchener?
  No. It was Mr. Toad!

The Queen and her Ladies-in-waiting
  Sat at the window and sewed.
She cried, 'Look! who's that *handsome* man?'
  They answered, 'Mr. Toad.'

Kenneth Grahame

Someone

Someone came knocking
At my wee, small door;
Someone came knocking,
I'm sure—sure—sure;
I listened, I opened,
I looked to left and right,
But nought there was a-stirring
In the still dark night.
Only the busy beetle
Tap-tapping in the wall,
Only from the forest
The screech-owl's call,
Only the cricket whistling
While the dewdrops fall,
So I know not who came knocking,
At all, at all, at all.

Walter de la Mare

The Fly

How large unto the tiny fly
  Must little things appear!—
A rosebud like a feather bed,
  Its prickle like a spear;

A dewdrop like a looking-glass,
  A hair like golden wire;
The smallest grain of mustard-seed
  As fierce as coals of fire;

A loaf of bread, a lofty hill;
  A wasp, a cruel leopard;
And specks of salt as bright to see
  As lambkins to a shepherd.

Walter de la Mare

Fairy Story

I went into the wood one day
And there I walked and lost my way

When it was so dark I could not see
A little creature came to me

He said if I would sing a song
The time would not be very long

But first I must let him hold my hand tight
Or else the wood would give me a fright

I sang a song, he let me go
But now I am home again there is nobody I know.

Stevie Smith

If Pigs Could Fly

If pigs could fly, I'd fly a pig
To foreign countries small and big—
To Italy and Spain,
To Austria, where cowbells ring,
To Germany, where people sing—
And then come home again.

I'd see the Ganges and the Nile;
I'd visit Madagascar's isle,
And Persia and Peru.
People would say they'd never seen
So odd, so strange an air-machine
As that on which I flew.

Why, everyone would raise a shout
To see his trotters and his snout
Come floating from the sky;
And I would be a famous star
Well known in countries near and far—
If only pigs could fly!

James Reeves

Windy Nights

Whenever the moon and stars are set,
  Whenever the wind is high,
All night long in the dark and wet,
  A man goes riding by.
Late in the night when the fires are out,
Why does he gallop and gallop about?

Whenever the trees are crying aloud,
  And ships are tossed at sea,
By, on the highway, low and loud,
  By at the gallop goes he.
By at the gallop he goes, and then
By he comes back at the gallop again.

Robert Louis Stevenson

The Signifying Monkey

The Monkey and the Lion
Got to talking one day.
Monkey looked down and said, 'Lion,
I hear you're king in every way.
But I know somebody
Who do not think that is true—
He told me he could whip
The living daylights out of you.'
Lion said, 'Who?'
Monkey said, 'Lion,
He talked about your mama
And talked about your grandma, too,
And I'm too polite to tell you
What he said about you.'
Lion said, 'Who said what? Who?'

Monkey in the tree,
Lion on the ground.
Monkey kept on signifying
But he didn't come down.
Monkey said, 'His name is Elephant—
He stone sure is not your friend.'
Lion said, 'He don't need to be
Because today will be his end.'
Lion took off through the jungle
Lickity-split,
Meaning to grab Elephant
And tear him bit to bit. Full stop!
He came across Elephant copping a righteous nod
Under a fine cool shady tree.
Lion said, 'You big old no-good so-and-so,
It's either you or me.'

Lion let out a solid roar
And bopped Elephant with his paw.
Elephant just took his trunk
And busted old Lion's jaw.
Lion let out another roar,
Reared up six feet tall.
Elephant just kicked him in the belly
And laughed to see him drop and fall.
Lion rolled over,
Copped Elephant by the throat.
Elephant just shook him loose
And butted him like a goat,
Then he tromped him and he stomped him
Till the Lion yelled, 'Oh, no!'
And it was near-nigh sunset
When Elephant let Lion go.

The signifying Monkey
Was still sitting in his tree
When he looked down and saw the Lion.
Said, 'Why, Lion, who can that there be?'
Lion said, 'Monkey, I don't want
To hear your jive-end jive.'
Monkey just kept on signifying,
'Lion, you for sure caught hell—
Mister Elephant's whipped you
To a fare-thee-well!
You ain't no king to me.
Fact is, I don't think that you
Can even as much as roar—
And if you try I'm liable
To come down out of this tree and
Whip your tail some more.'
The Monkey started laughing
And jumping up and down.

But he jumped so hard the limb broke
And he landed—bam!—on the ground.
When he went to run, his foot slipped
And he fell flat down.
Grrr-rrr-rr-r! The Lion was on him
With his front feet and his hind.
Monkey hollered, 'Ow!
I didn't mean it, Mister Lion!'
Lion said, 'You little flea-bag you!
Why, I'll eat you up alive.
I wouldn't a-been in this fix at all
Wasn't for your signifying jive.'
'Please,' said Monkey, 'Mister Lion,
If you'll just let me go,
I got something to tell you, please,
I think you ought to know.'

Lion let the Monkey loose
To see what his tale could be—
And Monkey jumped right back on up
Into his tree.
'What I was gonna tell you,' said Monkey,
'Is you square old so-and-so,
If you fool with me I'll get
Elephant to whip your head some more.'
'Monkey,' said the Lion,
Beat to his unbooted knees,
'You and all your signifying children
Better stay up in them trees.'
Which is why today
Monkey does his signifying
A-way-up out of the way.

Anonymous

In the Orchard

There was a giant by the Orchard Wall
Peeping about on this side and on that,
And feeling in the trees. He was as tall
As the big apple tree, and twice as fat:
His beard poked out, all bristly-black, and there
Were leaves and gorse and heather in his hair.

He held a blackthorn club in his right hand,
And plunged the other into every tree,
Searching for something—You could stand
Beside him and not reach up to his knee,
So big he was—I trembled lest he should
Come trampling, round-eyed, down to where I stood.

I tried to get away—But, as I slid
Under a bush, he saw me, and he bent
Down deep at me, and said, 'Where is she hid?'
I pointed over there, and off he went—

But, while he searched, I turned and simply flew
Round by the lilac bushes back to you.

James Stephens

The Walrus and the Carpenter

The sun was shining on the sea,
  Shining with all his might:
He did his very best to make
  The billows smooth and bright—
And this was odd, because it was
  The middle of the night.

The moon was shining sulkily,
  Because she thought the sun
Had got no business to be there
  After the day was done—
'It's very rude of him,' she said,
  'To come and spoil the fun!'

The sea was wet as wet could be,
  The sands were dry as dry.
You could not see a cloud, because
  No cloud was in the sky:
No birds were flying overhead—
  There were no birds to fly.

The Walrus and the Carpenter
  Were walking close at hand:
They wept like anything to see
  Such quantities of sand:
'If this were only cleared away,'
  They said, 'it *would* be grand!'

'If seven maids with seven mops
  Swept it for half a year,
Do you suppose,' the Walrus said,
  'That they could get it clear?'
'I doubt it,' said the Carpenter,
  And shed a bitter tear.

'O, Oysters, come and walk with us!'
    The Walrus did beseech.
'A pleasant walk, a pleasant talk,
    Along the briny beach:
We cannot do with more than four,
    To give a hand to each.'

The eldest Oyster looked at him,
    But never a word he said:
The eldest Oyster winked his eye,
    And shook his heavy head—
Meaning to say he did not choose
    To leave the oyster-bed.

But four young Oysters hurried up,
    All eager for the treat:
Their coats were brushed, their faces washed,
    Their shoes were clean and neat—
And this was odd, because, you know,
    They hadn't any feet.

Four other Oysters followed them,
    And yet another four;
And thick and fast they came at last,
    And more, and more, and more—
All hopping through the frothy waves,
    And scrambling to the shore.

The Walrus and the Carpenter
    Walked on a mile or so,
And then they rested on a rock
    Conveniently low:
And all the little Oysters stood
    And waited in a row.

'The time has come,' the Walrus said,
    'To talk of many things:
Of shoes—and ships—and sealing wax—
    Of cabbages—and kings—
And why the sea is boiling hot—
    And whether pigs have wings.'

'But wait a bit,' the Oysters cried,
    'Before we have our chat;
For some of us are out of breath,
    And all of us are fat!'
'No hurry!' said the Carpenter.
    They thanked him much for that.

'A loaf of bread,' the Walrus said,
    'Is what we chiefly need:
Pepper and vinegar besides
    Are very good indeed—
Now, if you're ready, Oysters dear,
    We can begin to feed.'

'But not on us!' the Oysters cried,
    Turning a little blue.
'After such kindness, that would be
    A dismal thing to do!'
'The night is fine,' the Walrus said.
    'Do you admire the view?

'It was so kind of you to come!
    And you are very nice!'
The Carpenter said nothing but
    'Cut us another slice.
I wish you were not quite so deaf—
    I've had to ask you twice!'

'It seems a shame,' the Walrus said,
    'To play them such a trick.
After we've brought them out so far,
    And made them trot so quick!'
The Carpenter said nothing but
    'The butter's spread too thick!'

'I weep for you,' the Walrus said:
  'I deeply sympathise.'
With sobs and tears he sorted out
  Those of the largest size,
Holding his pocket-handkerchief
  Before his streaming eyes.

'O, Oysters,' said the Carpenter,
  'You've had a pleasant run!
Shall we be trotting home again?'
  But answer came there none—
And this was scarcely odd, because
  They'd eaten every one.

Lewis Carroll

The Sugar-Plum Tree

Have you ever heard of the Sugar-Plum Tree?
   'Tis a marvel of great renown!
It blooms on the shore of the Lollipop sea
   In the garden of Shut-Eye Town;
The fruit that it bears is so wondrously sweet
   (As those who have tasted it say)
That good little children have only to eat
   Of that fruit to be happy next day.

When you've got to the tree, you would have a hard time
   To capture the fruit which I sing;
The tree is so tall that no person could climb
   To the boughs where the sugar-plums swing!
But up in that tree sits a chocolate cat,
   And a gingerbread dog prowls below—
And this is the way you contrive to get at
   Those sugar-plums tempting you so:

You say but the word to that gingerbread dog
   And he barks with such terrible zest
That the chocolate cat is at once all agog,
   As her swelling proportions attest.
And the chocolate cat goes cavorting around
   From this leafy limb unto that,
And the sugar-plums tumble, of course, to the ground—
   Hurrah for that chocolate cat!

There are marshmallows, gumdrops, and peppermint canes
   With stripings of scarlet or gold,
And you carry away of the treasure that rains
   As much as your apron can hold!
So come, little child, cuddle closer to me
   In your dainty white nightcap and gown,
And I'll rock you away to that Sugar-Plum Tree
   In the garden of Shut-Eye Town.

Eugene Field

110

Frutta di Mare

I am a sea shell flung
Up from the ancient sea;
Now I lie here, among
Roots of a tamarisk tree;
No one listens to me.

I sing to myself all day
In a husky voice, quite low,
Things the great fishes say
And you must need to know;
All night I sing just so.

But lift me from the ground,
And hearken at my rim;
Only your sorrow's sound
Amazed, perplexed and dim,
Comes coiling to the brim;

For what the wise whales ponder
Awaking out from sleep,
The key to all your wonder,
The answers of the deep,
These to myself I keep.

Geoffrey Scott

Eldorado

Gaily bedight,
A gallant knight,
In sunshine and in shadow,
Had journeyed long,
Singing a song,
In search of Eldorado.

But he grew old—
This knight so bold—
And o'er his heart a shadow
Fell, as he found
No spot of ground
That looked like Eldorado.

And, as his strength
Failed him at length,
He met a pilgrim shadow—
'Shadow,' said he,
'Where can it be—
This land of Eldorado?'

'Over the Mountains
Of the Moon,
Down the Valley of the Shadow,
Ride, boldly ride,'
The shade replied,
'If you seek for Eldorado!'

Edgar Allan Poe

My Mother Said

My mother said I never should
Play with the gypsies in the wood;
If I did, she would say,
Naughty girl to disobey.
Your hair shan't curl
And your shoes shan't shine,
You gypsy girl,
You shan't be mine.

And my father said that if I did
He'd rap my head with the tea-pot lid.
The wood was dark; the grass was green;
In came Sally with a tambourine.
I went to the sea—no ship to get across;
I paid ten shillings for a blind white horse;
I up on his back and was off in a crack,
Sally tell my mother I shall never come back.

Anonymous

My Dog Tray

On the green banks of Shannon when Sheelah was nigh,
No blithe Irish lad was so happy as I;
No harp like my own could so cheerily play,
And wherever I went was my poor dog Tray.

When at last I was forced from my Sheelah to part,
She said, (while the sorrow was big at her heart,)
Oh! remember your Sheelah when far, far away:
And be kind, my dear Pat, to our poor dog Tray.

Poor dog! he was faithful and kind to be sure,
And he constantly loved me although I was poor;
When the sour-looking folk sent me heartless away,
I had always a friend in my poor dog Tray.

When the road was so dark, and the night was so cold,
And Pat and his dog were grown weary and old,
How snugly we slept in my old coat of grey,
And he licked me for kindness—my old dog Tray.

Though my wallet was scant I remembered his case,
Nor refused my last crust to his pitiful face;
But he died at my feet on a cold winter day,
And I played a sad lament for my poor dog Tray.

Where now shall I go, poor, forsaken, and blind?
Can I find one to guide me, so faithful and kind?
To my sweet native village, so far, far away,
I can never more return with my poor dog Tray.

Thomas Campbell

Hallowe'en

This is the night when witches fly
On their whizzing broomsticks through the wintry sky;
Steering up the pathway where the stars are strewn,
They stretch skinny fingers to the waking moon.

This is the night when old wives tell
Strange and creepy stories, tales of charm and spell;
Peering at the pictures flaming in the fire
They wait for whispers from a ghostly choir.

This is the night when angels go
In and out the houses, winging o'er the snow;
Clearing out the demons from the countryside
They make it new and ready for Christmastide.

Leonard Clark

The Dark House

In a dark, dark wood, there was a dark, dark house,
And in that dark, dark house, there was a dark, dark room,
And in that dark, dark room, there was a dark, dark cupboard,
And in that dark, dark cupboard, there was a dark, dark shelf,
And in that dark, dark shelf, there was a dark, dark box,
And in that dark, dark box, there was a GHOST!

Anonymous

Jack Frost

The door was shut, as doors should be,
Before you went to bed last night;
But Jack Frost has got in, you see,
And left your window silver white.

He must have waited till you slept;
And not a single word he spoke,
But pencilled o'er the panes and crept
Away again before you woke.

And now you cannot see the hills
Nor fields that stretch beyond the lane;
But there are fairer things than these
His fingers traced on every pane.

Rocks and castles towering high;
Hills and dales and streams and fields;
And knights in armour riding by,
With nodding plumes and shining shields.

And here are little boats, and there
Big ships with sails spread to the breeze;
And yonder, palm trees waving fair
On islands set in silver seas.

And butterflies with gauzy wings;
And herds of cows and flocks of sheep;
And fruit and flowers and all the things
You see when you are sound asleep.

For creeping softly underneath
The door, when all the lights are out,
Jack Frost takes every breath you breathe
And knows the things you think about.

He paints them on the window pane,
In fairy lines with frozen steam;
And when you wake you see again
The lovely things you saw in dream.

Gabriel Setoun

The Rainbow Fairies

Two little clouds, one summer's day,
Went flying through the sky;
They went so fast they bumped their heads,
And both began to cry.

Old Father Sun looked out and said:
'Oh, never mind, my dears,
I'll send my little fairy folk
To dry your falling tears.'

One fairy came in violet,
And one wore indigo;
In blue, green, yellow, orange, red,
They made a pretty row.

They wiped the cloud-tears all away,
And then from out the sky,
Upon a line the sunbeams made,
They hung their gowns to dry.

Anonymous

120

The Little Things That Happen

The Little Things That Happen
    Are tucked into your mind,
And come again to greet you
    (Or most of them, you'll find).

Through many little doorways,
    Of which you keep the keys,
They crowd into your thinking—
    We call them Memories.

But some of them are rovers
    And wander off and get
So lost, the keys grow rusty,
    And that means—you forget.

But some stay ever near you;
    You'll find they never rove—
The keys are always shining—
    Those are the things you love.

Marjorie Wilson

A Night with a Wolf

High up on the lonely mountains,
　　Where the wild men watched and waited;
Wolves in the forest, and bears in the bush,
　　And I on my path belated.

The rain and the night together
　　Came down, and the wind came after,
Bending the props of the pine-tree roof,
　　And snapping many a rafter.

I crept along in the darkness,
　　Stunned, and bruised, and blinded;
Crept to a fir with thick-set boughs,
　　And a sheltering rock behind it.

There, from the blowing and raining,
　　Crouching, I sought to hide me.
Something rustled; two green eyes shone;
　　And a wolf lay down beside me!

His wet fur pressed against me;
　　Each of us warmed the other;
Each of us felt, in the stormy dark,
　　That beast and man were brother.

And when the falling forest
　　No longer crashed in warning,
Each of us went from our hiding place
　　Forth in the wild, wet morning.

Bayard Taylor

A Kitten

He's nothing much but fur
And two round eyes of blue,
He has a giant purr
And a midget mew.

He darts and pats the air,
He starts and pricks his ear,
When there is nothing there
For him to see and hear.

He runs around in rings,
But why we cannot tell;
With sideways leap he springs
At things invisible—

Then half-way through a leap
His startled eyeballs close,
And he drops off to sleep
With one paw on his nose.

Eleanor Farjeon

The Owl and the Pussy-Cat

The Owl and the Pussy-Cat went to sea
In a beautiful pea-green boat,
They took some honey, and plenty of money,
Wrapped up in a five-pound note.
The Owl looked up to the stars above,
And sang to a small guitar,
'O lovely Pussy! O Pussy, my love,
What a beautiful Pussy you are,
You are,
You are!
What a beautiful Pussy you are!'

Pussy said to the Owl, 'You elegant fowl!
    How charmingly sweet you sing!
O let us be married! too long we have tarried:
    But what shall we do for a ring?'
They sailed away, for a year and a day,
    To the land where the Bong-Tree grows,
And there in a wood a Piggy-wig stood,
    With a ring at the end of his nose,
        His nose,
        His nose,
    With a ring at the end of his nose.

'Dear Pig, are you willing to sell for one shilling
    Your ring?' Said the Piggy, 'I will.'
So they took it away, and were married next day
    By the Turkey who lives on the hill.
They dined on mince, and slices of quince,
    Which they ate with a runcible spoon;
And hand in hand, on the edge of the sand,
    They danced by the light of the moon,
        The moon,
        The moon,
    They danced by the light of the moon.

Edward Lear

The White Sea-gull

The white sea-gull, the wild sea-gull!
　A joyful bird is he,
As he lies like a cradled thing at rest
　In the arms of a sunny sea!
The little waves wash to and fro,
　And the white gull lies asleep;
As the fisher's boat with breeze and tide,
　Goes merrily over the deep,
The ship, with her sails set, goes by;
　And her people stand to note
How the sea-gull sits on the rocking waves,
　As still as an anchored boat.
The sea is fresh, and the sea is fair,
　And the sky calm overhead;
And the sea-gull lies on the deep, deep sea,
　Like a king in his royal bed!

Mary Howitt

The Robin

When up aloft
I fly and fly,
I see in pools
The shining sky,
And a happy bird
Am I, am I!

When I descend
Toward the brink
I stand and look
And stop and drink
And bathe my wings,
And chink, and prink.

When winter frost
Makes earth as steel,
I search and search
But find no meal,
And most unhappy
Then I feel.

But when it lasts,
And snows still fall,
I get to feel
No grief at all,
For I turn to a cold, stiff
Feathery ball!

Thomas Hardy

It Was Long Ago

I'll tell you, shall I, something I remember?
Something that still means a great deal to me.
It was long ago.

A dusty road in summer I remember,
A mountain, and an old house, and a tree
That stood, you know,

Behind the house. An old woman I remember
In a red shawl with a grey cat on her knee
Humming under a tree.

She seemed the oldest thing I can remember,
But then perhaps I was not more than three.
It was long ago.

I dragged on the dusty road, and I remember
How the old woman looked over the fence at me
And seemed to know

How it felt to be three, and called out, I remember
'Do you like bilberries and cream for tea?'
I went under the tree

And while she hummed, and the cat purred,
    I remember
How she filled a saucer with berries and cream for me
So long ago,

Such berries and such cream as I remember
I never had seen before, and never see
Today, you know.

And that is almost all I can remember,
The house, the mountain, the grey cat on her knee,
Her red shawl, and the tree,

And the taste of the berries, the feel of the sun
    I remember,
And the smell of everything that used to be
So long ago,

Till the heat on the road outside again I remember,
And how the long dusty road seemed to have for me
No end, you know.

That is the farthest thing I can remember.
It won't mean much to you. It does to me.
Then I grew up, you see.

Eleanor Farjeon

Answer to a Child's Question

Do you ask what the birds say? The Sparrow, the Dove,
The Linnet and Thrush say, 'I love and I love!'
In the winter they're silent—the wind is so strong;
What it says, I don't know, but it sings a loud song.
But green leaves, and blossoms, and sunny warm
   weather,
And singing, and loving—all come back together.
But the Lark is so brimful of gladness and love,
The green fields below him, the blue sky above,
That he sings, and he sings: and for ever sings he—
'I love my Love, and my Love loves me!'

Samuel Taylor Coleridge

The Sound of the Wind

The wind has such a rainy sound
   Moaning through the town,
The sea has such a windy sound—
   Will the ships go down?

The apples in the orchard
   Tumble from their tree—
Oh will the ships go down, go down,
   In the windy sea?

Christina Rossetti

The Pobble
who has No Toes

The Pobble who has no toes
    Had once as many as we;
When they said, 'Some day you may lose them all'—
    He replied, 'Fish fiddle de-dee!'
And his Aunt Jobiska made him drink,
Lavender water tinged with pink,
For she said, 'The World in general knows
There's nothing so good for a Pobble's toes!'

The Pobble who has no toes,
    Swam across the Bristol Channel;
But before he set out he wrapped his nose
    In a piece of scarlet flannel.
For his Aunt Jobiska said, 'No harm
Can come to his toes if his nose is warm;
And it's perfectly known that a Pobble's toes
Are safe—provided he minds his nose.'

The Pobble swam fast and well,
    And when boats or ships came near him
He tinkledy-binkledy-winkled a bell,
    So that all the world could hear him.
And all the Sailors and Admirals cried,
When they saw him nearing the further side—
'He has gone to fish, for his Aunt Jobiska's
Runcible Cat with crimson whiskers!'

But before he touched the shore,
    The shore of the Bristol Channel,
A sea-green Porpoise carried away
    His wrapper of scarlet flannel.
And when he came to observe his feet,
Formerly garnished with toes so neat,
His face at once became forlorn
On perceiving that all his toes were gone!

And nobody ever knew
    From that dark day to the present,
Whoso had taken the Pobble's toes,
    In a manner so far from pleasant.
Whether the shrimps or crawfish grey,
Or crafty Mermaids stole them away—
Nobody knew; and nobody knows
How the Pobble was robbed of his twice five toes!

The Pobble who has no toes
    Was placed in a friendly Bark,
And they rowed him back, and carried him up,
    To his Aunt Jobiska's Park.
And she made him a feast at his earnest wish
Of eggs and buttercups fried with fish—
And she said—'It's a fact the whole world knows,
That Pobbles are happier without their toes.'

Edward Lear

The Little Wee Man

As I was walking all alone
Between a river and a wall,
There I saw a little wee man—
I'd never seen a man so small.

His legs were barely a finger long,
His shoulders wide as fingers three;
Light and springing was his step,
And he stood lower than my knee.

He lifted a stone six feet high,
He lifted it up to his right knee,
Above his chest, above his head,
And flung it as far as I could see.

'O,' said I, 'how strong you are!
I wonder where your home can be.'
'Down the green valley there;
O will you come with me and see?'

So on we ran, and away we rode,
Until we came to his bonny home;
The roof was made of beaten gold,
The floor was made of crystal stone.

Pipers were playing, ladies dancing,
Four-and-twenty ladies gay;
And as they danced they were singing,
'Our little wee man's been long away.'

Ian Serraillier

A Fairy Went A-Marketing

A Fairy went a-marketing—
   She bought a little fish;
She put it in a crystal bowl
   Upon a golden dish.
An hour she sat in wonderment
   And watched its silver gleam,
And then she gently took it up
   And slipped it in a stream.

A fairy went a-marketing—
   She bought a coloured bird;
It sang the sweetest, shrillest song
   That ever she had heard,
She sat beside its painted cage
   And listened half the day,
And then she opened wide the door
   And let it fly away.

A fairy went a-marketing—
   She bought a winter gown
All stitched about with gossamer
   And lined with thistledown.
She wore it all the afternoon
   With prancing and delight,
Then gave it to a little frog
   To keep him warm at night.

A fairy went a-marketing—
   She bought a gentle mouse
To take her tiny messages,
   To keep her little house.
All day she kept its busy feet
   Pit-patting to and fro,
And then she kissed its silken ears,
   Thanked it, and let it go.

Rose Fyleman

135

The Rock-a-By Lady

The Rock-a-By Lady from Hushaby street
   Comes stealing; comes creeping;
The poppies they hang from her head to her feet,
And each hath a dream that is tiny and fleet—
She bringeth her poppies to you, my sweet,
   When she findeth you sleeping!

There is one little dream of a beautiful drum—
   'Rub-a-dub!' it goeth;
There is one little dream of a big sugar-plum,
And lo! thick and fast the other dreams come
Of popguns that bang, and tin tops that hum,
   And a trumpet that bloweth!

And dollies peep out of those wee little dreams
   With laughter and singing;
And boats go a-floating on silvery streams,
And the stars peek-a-boo with their own misty gleams,
And up, up, and up, where the Mother Moon beams,
   The fairies go winging!

Would you dream all these dreams that are tiny and fleet?
   They'll come to you sleeping;
So shut the two eyes that are weary, my sweet,
For the Rock-a-By Lady from Hushaby street,
With poppies that hang from her head to her feet,
   Comes stealing; comes creeping.

Eugene Field

The North Wind Doth Blow

The north wind doth blow,
And we shall have snow,
And what will the robin do then, poor thing?
　　He'll sit in a barn,
　　And keep himself warm,
And hide his head under his wing, poor thing!

The north wind doth blow,
And we shall have snow,
And what will the swallow do then, poor thing?
　　Oh, do you not know
　　That he's off long ago,
To a country where he will find spring, poor thing!

The north wind doth blow,
And we shall have snow,
And what will the dormouse do then, poor thing?
　　Roll'd up like a ball,
　　In his nest snug and small,
He'll sleep till warm weather comes in, poor thing!

The north wind doth blow,
And we shall have snow,
And what will the honey-bee do then, poor thing?
   In his hive he will stay
   Till the cold is away,
And then he'll come out in the spring, poor thing!

The north wind doth blow,
And we shall have snow,
And what will the children do then, poor things?
   When lessons are done,
   They must skip, jump and run,
Until they have made themselves warm, poor things!

Anonymous

139

An Eskimo Baby

If you were an Eskimo baby
You'd live in a bag all day.
   Right up from your toes
   To the tip of your nose,
All in thick cosy furs tucked away.

And if you went out for an airing
In mother's warm hood you would go,
   Tied close to her back,
   Like a soft, furry pack,
You could laugh at the cold and the snow.

But if they brought water at bedtime—
As people at home always do—
   You'd cough and you'd sneeze,
   And perhaps you would freeze,
You would certainly turn very blue!

An Eskimo mummy would rub you
With oil from your heels to your head.
   And then you'd be rolled
   (For it's terribly cold)
In warm furs, and put safely to bed.

No nice creamy milk for your supper,
But bits of raw blubber and fat!
   Would you like to go
   To the land of the snow,
Where they have such a bedtime as that?

Lucy Diamond

The Kayak

Over the briny wave I go,
In spite of the weather, in spite of the snow:
What cares the hardy Eskimo?
In my little skiff, with paddle and lance,
I glide where the foaming billows dance.

Round me the sea-birds slip and soar;
Like me, they love the oceans' roar.
Sometimes a floating iceberg gleams
Above me with its melting streams;
Sometimes a rushing wave will fall
Down on my skiff and cover it all.

But what care I for a wave's attack?
With my paddle I right my little kayak,
And then its weight I speedily trim,
And over the water away I skim.

Anonymous

The Kitten
in the Falling Snow

The year-old kitten
has never seen snow,
fallen or falling, until now
this late winter afternoon.

He sits with wide eyes
at the firelit window, sees
white things falling
from black trees.

Are they petals, leaves or birds?
They cannot be the cabbage whites
he batted briefly with his paws,
or the puffball seeds in summer grass.

They make no sound, they have no wings
and yet they can whirl and fly around
until they swoop like swallows, and
disappear into the ground.

'Where do they go?' he questions,
with eyes ablaze, following their flight
into black stone. So I put him
out into the yard, to make their acquaintance.

He has to look up at them: when one
blanches his coral nose, he sneezes,
and flicks a few from his whiskers, from
his sharpened ear, that picks up silences.

He catches one on a curled-up paw
and licks it quickly, before
its strange milk fades, then sniffs its ghost,
a wetness, while his black coat

shivers with stars of flickering frost.
He shivers at something else that makes his thin
tail swish, his fur stand on end! 'What's this? . . .'
Then he suddenly scoots in to safety

and sits again with wide eyes
at the firelit window, sees
white things falling
from black trees.

James Kirkup

Travel

I should like to rise and go
Where the golden apples grow;
Where below another sky
Parrot islands anchored lie,
And, watched by cockatoos and goats,
Lonely Crusoes building boats;
Where in sunshine reaching out
Eastern cities, miles about,
Are with mosque and minaret
Among sandy gardens set,
And the rich goods from near and far
Hang for sale in the bazaar;
Where the Great Wall round China goes,
And on one side the desert blows,
And with bell and voice and drum,
Cities on the other hum;
Where are forests, hot as fire,
Wide as England, tall as a spire,
Full of apes and coconuts
And the negro hunters' huts;
Where the knotty crocodile
Lies and blinks in the Nile,
And the red flamingo flies
Hunting fish before his eyes;
Where in jungles, near and far,
Man-devouring tigers are,
Lying close and giving ear
Lest the hunt be drawing near,
Or a comer-by be seen
Swinging in a palanquin;

Where among the desert sands
Some deserted city stands,
All its children, sweep and prince,
Grown to manhood ages since,
Not a foot in street or house,
Not a stir of child or mouse,
And when kindly falls the night,
In all the town no spark of light.
There I'll come when I'm a man
With a camel caravan;
Light a fire in the gloom
Of some dusty dining-room;
See the pictures on the walls,
Heroes, fights and festivals;
And in a corner find the toys
Of the old Egyptian boys.

Robert Louis Stevenson

Three Jolly Huntsmen

Three jolly huntsmen,
I've heard people say,
Went hunting together
On St David's Day.

All day they hunted,
And nothing could they find,
But a ship a-sailing,
A-sailing with the wind.

One said it was a ship,
The other he said, Nay;
The third said it was a house,
With the chimney blown away.

And all the night they hunted,
And nothing could they find
But the moon a-gliding
A-gliding with the wind.

One said it was the moon,
The other he said, Nay;
The third said it was a cheese,
And a half of it cut away.

And all the day they hunted,
And nothing did they find
But a hedgehog in a bramble-bush,
And that they left behind.

The first said it was a hedgehog,
The second he said, Nay;
The third said it was a pin cushion,
And the pins stuck in wrong way.

And all the night they hunted,
And nothing could they find
But a hare in a turnip-field,
And that they left behind.

The first said it was a hare,
The second he said, Nay;
The third said it was a calf,
And the cow had run away.

And all the day they hunted,
And nothing could they find
But an owl in a holly-tree,
And that they left behind.

One said it was an owl,
The second he said, Nay;
The third said 'twas an old man,
And his beard was growing gray.

Anonymous

The Pig's Tail

A furry coat has the bear to wear,
  The tortoise a coat of mail,
The yak has more than his share of hair,
  But—the pig has the curly tail.

The elephant's tusks are sold for gold,
  The slug leaves a silver trail,
The parrot is never too old to scold,
  But—the pig has a curly tail.

The lion can either roar or snore,
  The cow gives milk in a pail,
The dog can guard a door, and more,
  But—the pig has the curly tail.

The monkey makes you smile a while,
  The tiger makes you quail,
The fox has many a wile of guile,
  But—the pig has the curly tail.

For the rest of the beasts that prey or play,
  From tiny mouse to the whale,
There's much that I could say today,
  But—the pig has the curly tail.

Norman Ault

Ducks' Ditty

All along the backwater,
Through the rushes tall,
Ducks are a-dabbling,
Up tails all!

Ducks' tails, drakes' tails,
Yellow feet a-quiver,
Yellow bills all out of sight
Busy in the river!

Slushy green undergrowth
Where the roach swim—
Here we keep our larder,
Cool and full and dim.

Every one for what he likes!
We like to be
Heads down, tails up,
Dabbling free!

High in the blue above
Swifts whirl and call—
We are down a-dabbling,
Up tails all!

Kenneth Grahame

The Squirrel

Among the fox-red fallen leaves I surprised him. Snap
Up the chestnut bole he leapt,
The brown leaper, clawing up-swept:
Turned on the first bough and scolded me roundly.
That's right, load me with reviling,
Spit at me, swear horrible, shame me if you can.
But scared of my smiling
Off and up he scurries. Now Jack's up the beanstalk
Among the dizzy giants. He skips
Along the highest branches, along
Tree-fingers slender as string,
Fur tail following, to the very tips:
Then leaps the aisle—
Oh fear he fall
A hundred times his little length!
He's over! clings, swings on a spray,
Then lightly, the ghost of a mouse, against the sky traces
For me his runway of rare wonder, races
Helter-skelter without pause or break
(I think of the snail—how long would he take?)
On and onward, not done yet—
His errand? Some nut-plunder, you bet.
Oh he's gone!
I peer and search and strain for him, but he's gone.

I wait and watch at the giants' feet, among
The fox-red fallen leaves. One drop
Of rain lands with a smart tap
On the drum, on parchment leaf. I wait
And wait and shiver and forget . . .

A fancy: suppose these trees, so ancient, so
Venerable, so rock-rooted, suddenly
Heaved up their huge elephantine hooves
(O the leaves, how they'd splutter and splash
Like a waterfall, a red waterfall)—suppose
They trudged away!
What would the squirrel say?

Ian Serraillier

A Smugglers' Song

If you wake at midnight and hear a horse's feet,
Don't go drawing back the blind, or looking in the
  street,
Them that asks no questions isn't told a lie.
Watch the wall, my darling, while the Gentlemen
  go by!
     Five and twenty ponies,
     Trotting through the dark—
     Brandy for the Parson,
     'Baccy for the Clerk;
     Laces for a lady; letters for a spy,
And watch the wall, my darling, while the Gentlemen
  go by!

Running round the woodlump if you chance to find
Little barrels, roped and tarred, all full of brandy-wine;
Don't you shout to come and look, nor take 'em for
  your play;
Put the brushwood back again—and they'll be gone
  next day!

If you see the stableyard setting open wide;
If you see a tired horse lying down inside;
If your mother mends a coat cut about and tore;
If the lining's wet and warm—don't you ask no more!

If you meet King George's men, dressed in blue and
  red,
You be careful what you say, and mindful what is said.
If they call you 'pretty maid', and chuck you 'neath the
  chin,
Don't you tell where no one is, nor yet where no one's
  been!

Knocks and footsteps round the house—whistles after
  dark—
You've no call for running out till the housedogs bark.
Trusty's here and Pincher's here, and see how dumb
  they lie—
They don't fret to follow when the Gentlemen go by!

If you do as you've been told, likely there's a chance,
You'll be give a dainty doll, all the way from France,
With a cap of Valenciennes, and a velvet hood—
A present from the Gentlemen, along o' being good!
        Five and twenty ponies,
        Trotting through the dark—
        Brandy for the Parson,
        'Baccy for the Clerk.
Them that asks no questions isn't told a lie—
Watch the wall, my darling, while the Gentlemen
  go by!

Rudyard Kipling

Sweet and Low

Sweet and low, sweet and low,
Wind of the Western sea.
Low, low, breathe and blow,
Wind of the Western sea.
Over the rolling waters go,
Come from the dying moon, and blow,
Blow him again to me;
While my little one, while my pretty one sleeps.

Sleep and rest, sleep and rest,
Father will come to thee soon;
Rest, rest, on mother's breast,
Father will come to thee soon;
Father will come to his babe in the nest,
Silver sails all out of the west
Under the silver moon;
Sleep my little one, sleep my pretty one, sleep.

Alfred, Lord Tennyson

Index of First Lines

Acknowledgements

We wish to thank the following for permission to use copyright poems:

Norman Ault: *The Pig's Tail* from *Dreamland Shores* (1920) by permission of Oxford University Press. **Walter de la Mare:** *Silver, Someone* and *The Fly* by permission of The Literary Trustees of Walter de la Mare and The Society of Authors as their representative. **Eleanor Farjeon:** *The Night Will Never Stay, A Kitten, It Was Long Ago* and *Cat!* from *Silver Sand and Snow*, published by Michael Joseph by permission of David Higham Associates Ltd. **Rose Fyleman:** *The Balloon Man, Fairies* and *A Fairy Went a – Marketing* from *Fairies and Chimneys* by permission of The Society of Authors as the literary representative of the estate of Rose Fyleman. **Percy Ilott:** *The Witch* from *Songs of English Childhood* by permission of J. M. Dent & Sons Ltd. **James Kirkup:** *The Lonely Scarecrow* and *Kitten In The Falling Snow* from *Refusal to Conform* by permission of Mr James Kirkup and Oxford University Press. **Rudyard Kipling:** *A Smugglers' Song* from the *Definitive Edition of Rudyard Kipling's Verse* by permission of The National Trust for Places of Historic Interest or Natural Beauty and Macmillan and Co Ltd, London. **John Masefield:** *Sea Fever* by permission of The Society of Authors as the literary representative of the estate of John Masefield and of Macmillan Publishing Company (New York Macmillan, 1953). **Roger McGough:** *Mrs Moon* from *Sky In The Pie* reprinted by permission of A. D. Peters and Co Ltd. **Spike Milligan:** *On The Ning Nang Nong* by permission of Spike Milligan Productions Ltd. **Ogden Nash:** *The Duck* from *Verses from 1929 On* © 1936 by the Curtis Publishing Company, first appeared in the Saturday Evening Post, by permission of Andre Deutsch Ltd and Little Brown and Co, Boston, USA. **Alfred Noyes:** *The Highwayman* by permission of Blackwood Pillans & Wilson. **Jack Prelutsky:** *The Hippopotamus* from *Zoo Doings* © 1970, 1983 by Jack Prelutsky by permission of Greenwillow Books (A Division of William Morrow & Company). **James Reeves:** *If Pigs Could Fly* from *James Reeves – The Complete Poems* by permission of Laura Cecil for and on behalf of James Reeves' Estate. Reprinted by permission of the James Reeves Estate. **Alexander Resnikoff:** *Two Witches* from *Oh, How Silly!* by permission of Laurence Pollinger Ltd. **Theodore Roethke:** *The Serpent* © 1950 from the book, *The Collected Poems of Theodore Roethke* reprinted by permission of Doubleday and Co Inc, and Faber and Faber Ltd. **Clive Sansom:** *The Witches' Call* from *The Golden Unicorn* published by Methuen Books Ltd by permission of David Higham Associates Ltd. **Ian Serraillier:** *The Little Wee Man* from *I'll Tell You A Tale* © 1973–1976 and *The Squirrel* from *A Puffin Quartet of Poets* 1944, 1958, © Ian Serraillier, Puffin Books Ltd. **Gabriel Setoun:** *Romance* and *Jack Frost* by permission of The Bodley Head Ltd from *The Child World* by Gabriel Setoun, **Osbert Sitwell:** *Winter The Huntsman* from *Selected Poems* by permission of Duckworth and Co Ltd and David Higham Associates Ltd. **Stevie Smith:** *Fairy Story* from *The Collected Poems* © 1972 by Stevie Smith (Penguin Modern Classics) by permission of James MacGibbon as The Literary Executor and by permission of New Directions Publishing Corp. **Marjorie Wilson:** *The Little Things That Happen* by permission of Basil Blackwell. **Raymond Wilson:** *The Traveller* from *Times Delight* © Raymond Wilson.

Every effort has been made to trace copyright holders but this has not been possible in every case. The publishers apologise to any copyright holders whose rights have been unwittingly infringed.